Business Finance 101
Monopolies, Accounting, Audits, and Blockchain

Louis Bevoc

Published by
NutriNiche System LLC

Louis Bevoc books...simple explanations of complex subjects

Monopolies	3
Accounting	17
Audits	28
Blockchain	42

Monopolies in Business
A Basic Introduction

Louis Bevoc

Published by
NutriNiche System LLC

Louis Bevoc books...simple explanations of complex subjects

Introduction — 6
Causes — 6
- Volume — 6
- Cost — 7
- Brand loyalty — 7
- Licensing — 7
- Mergers and acquisitions — 7
- Size and location — 8
- Common sense — 8
- Government — 8

Effects — 9
- Price — 9
- Supply — 9
- Demand — 9
- Efficiency — 10
- Innovation — 10
- Strategy — 10
- Bankruptcy — 10

Advantages — 11
- Profit — 11
- Name brand recognition — 11
- Technology — 11
- Honesty — 12
- Pricing — 12

Disadvantages — 12
- Exploitation — 12
- Wealth distribution — 13
- Quality — 13
- Bullying — 13
- Worker wages — 13

Methods of regulation — 14
- Mandate price controls — 14
- Transform private assets into public assets — 14
- Break up organizations — 14
- Merger and acquisition policies — 15

Price monitoring 15
Service monitoring 15
Summary 16

Introduction

The word "monopoly" is often associated with a board game that has been a part of American culture since 1935. Players buy properties, houses, and hotels with the ultimate goal being to "monopolize" their opponents by driving them into bankruptcy. This board game association is understandable, but it is not the focus of this book. Instead, this book examines monopolies in the real world. More specifically, it discusses the causes, effects, advantages, disadvantages, and regulations of monopolies in business.

For simplification purposes, this book defines monopolies in business as:

> Unrestricted control of the supply and sale of products and/or services

In regard to this definition, other organizations have the freedom to enter into competition with monopolizing businesses. However, those organizations are prevented from becoming true competitors due to factors controlled by the monopolies including price, supply, patents, and technology. For this reason, government agencies enact policies that curtail monopolist control...and those policies will be discussed later in this book.

In the United States, large-scale monopolies are few and far between. In fact, it is difficult to find a market where some form of competition does not exist. Some would argue that Microsoft and Facebook fall into the monopoly category, but they actually do have competition. Companies of the past like AT&T and Standard Oil are better examples of organizations that had monopolistic tendencies.

Now that you have a basic understanding of the scope of this book, let's move on to a discussion on the reasons that monopolies occur.

Causes

What causes a business to become a monopoly? This is a good question because the answer is detailed and requires a wealth of information to properly understand. However, the basic reason that monopolies develop is that circumstances prevent other organizations from competing in the same market. These circumstances often involve control of physical or intellectual resources. An example showing physical resource control is a food company that owns 90 percent of the pecan farms in the United States. This ownership of land allows them to control the price and quantity of pecans sold to manufacturers and distributors. Along the same lines, an example of intellectual resource control is a pharmaceutical company that has a patent on a cancer-fighting drug. They control the price and distribution of this medicine until their patent runs out.

In addition to controlling resources, other factors produce monopolies by reducing or eliminating competition. These factors include:

Volume

The old saying "there is safety in numbers" has application in business. Those numbers refer to the volume of goods sold by an organization. Higher numbers of goods sold result in greater control of markets because unit costs are lowered, thereby increasing profitability for the selling organizations. Higher profits allow for reinvestment in a new market, and the cycle repeats itself. Over time, that market is flooded with one company's products, there is little room for competition, and a monopoly results.

Cost

As noted above, cost is related to volume because it can be lowered as higher numbers of goods are sold. However, cost is also lower for some companies before any products are sold due to the capability and track record of that company. For example, a large food manufacturer that sells vegetables all over the United States is able to negotiate very low prices on flour for a new pasta line they are developing. They are given this price because they have established sales nationwide, and they already have distribution in place for the new pasta line. In this sense, they have the ability to produce a cost-related monopoly before they sell their first package of product. This might seem unfair…but it is reality in some situations.

Brand loyalty

Brand loyalty can cause monopolies because people require a particular product or service regardless of the price or volume. They want a certain brand, and they will not settle for any replacement. They will even go out of their way to acquire that brand…and this prevents other organizations from competing. An example of a brand with the potential to monopolize is Corvette. Some people want to own a Corvette, and another type of automobile is not acceptable.

Believe it or not, some organizations have concerns about brand loyalty hurting them. For example, many people refer to all facial tissue as "Kleenex," even though it is a brand name. If this reference becomes too common and a monopoly develops, the government can step in to break up the company to promote competition.

Licensing

Licensing is similar to patents in the regard that it is limited to a certain time period. Like patents, licenses give organizations exclusivity to a product or service without the threat of competition. Licenses are often granted by the government along with regulations that must be followed. In addition to time limits, these regulations also include geographical areas where the licensing is applicable. Essentially, licensing creates "controlled" monopolies that exist in designated areas and expire over time.

Mergers and acquisitions

When two large companies become one, there is a threat of a sudden monopoly developing. This is because quite often the merging organizations are competitors, and they both control part or most of the same market. Antitrust laws prevent some mega-mergers from dominating the marketplace, but these laws are not foolproof. Add to this the fact that the combined resources and leadership of the merging companies might be the best in the industry, and it is relatively easy to see how competition can be restricted.

Size and location

When markets are small or isolated, there is a better chance for a monopoly to exist. This is due to the limited choices available in those markets. For example, people in a small town might buy all of their electronics from one store because it is the only store in town that carries electronics. However, a monopoly caused by size and location had a much better chance of existing in the past than it does today due to the online choices available to consumers. The internet brings products and services to people's doorsteps, thereby opening up a competitive market for most items. That being said, it must be remembered that the internet is not a complete solution for lack of competition. For example, the internet probably does not affect the control that a sole dental office has in a small town. People cannot get their teeth fixed online...so they use the local dentist.

Common sense

This factor might be the least well-known to the average person. Some monopolies exist simply because they are the best method available for accomplishing goals and objectives. Utilities are a good example of market domination that occurs as a result of common sense. Constructing duplicate or competing water pipes, electrical cables, or gas lines increases prices for consumers and destroys the environment. It makes much more sense to have a few isolated organizations providing these services, and there is typically little objection to this type of arrangement.

Professional sports teams are another example of this type of monopoly. For example, the Toronto Maple Leafs franchise is an NHL team that dominates the Toronto area hockey fan base. Another team can try to compete, but it would be very difficult based on the money, time, and effort required. It makes more sense to only have one team in Toronto that all fans support, and there is little objection to this type of arrangement.

Government

Government is the only area where monopolies are completely accepted...and even expected in many instances. For example, the IRS is the only organization that can tax people and businesses in the United States. This government agency is a monopoly that has no competition, and its status is considered acceptable. Another example is the police department in a city. Police officers are the only people legally authorized to enforce rules and regulations, and this is acceptable to everyone in the community (and those in the federal government).

Regardless of the reason why monopolies exist, they are present in some forms and will likely continue to be a part of most societies. This is because rewards come with monopolizing markets. Those rewards are typically in the form of profitability, and the individuals on the receiving end of those profits benefit handsomely. Leaders put their organizations at risk when they approach monopoly status...but that risk appears to be well worth the reward.

Now that you understand some of the major causes of monopolies, we need to explore what happens after they come into being. The next section discusses the effects of monopolization of markets.

Effects

As noted in the introduction, a monopoly in business is defined as "unrestricted control of the supply and sale of products and/or services." It exists when there is only one seller of a product or service in a particular market, and barriers are put up to prevent the entry of competitors. When this happens, the impact is felt in a variety of different ways. Customers and businesses are affected, and, if left uncontrolled, the situation becomes a legal issue that requires government intervention.

The following are affected by a monopoly:

Price

Most companies monitor the pricing of their competitors to justify the value of their own products or services. Quality plays a role here because high-quality goods and services allow for higher prices, but there is a ceiling based on prices set by other companies in the same market. However, this thinking about pricing changes when there is a monopoly. Organizations that control markets have the freedom to change prices without worrying about competition. As long as there is a demand, they can charge customers more money without fear of being undercut by another organization in the same market. The lack of choices puts consumers at the mercy of the monopoly, and this is the exact opposite of what is supposed to happen.

Price is an interesting concept because sometimes it is intended to help people make the choice not to buy a product. This strategy might appear to contradict itself, but it actually makes good sense in certain situations. For example, the United States government places a huge tax on cigarettes, thereby driving up the consumer price to levels astronomically higher than the cost to produce them. No other organization can control cigarette taxes, so this is a monopolistic activity. However, the price increase is meant to stop consumers from smoking and damaging their health…so it makes sense to most people.

Supply

A business monopoly is able to control the supply of its product or service because it has no competition. By limiting supply, they can create a higher demand…and raise the price accordingly. For example, a computer software manufacturer with a hot new product can limit supply, thereby driving up demand. They can then raise the price, and people will pay it just to obtain the product. This is unfair to the consumer, but the low supply makes them feel good about having the software, and it justifies the price increase in their minds.

Demand

As supply decreases, demand increases, causing the monopoly to solidify itself. More people want the product or service, and the monopoly benefits profoundly. A real-world example is Facebook. People want to communicate with each other via social media, and Facebook monopolizes the need. There are other forms of social media for communication, but most people are on Facebook, so the demand for its services increases…and Facebook profits very handsomely.

Efficiency

Organizations that monopolize a product or service often become complacent. They have no competition, so there is no reason to become more efficient to get better. In other words, they do not actively seek out improvement like companies that compete against other businesses that are continually upgrading. Competitive markets require the companies in them to reduce costs and prices to gain market share...but this is not a priority for monopolizing organizations.

Innovation

Similar to efficiency, monopolizing organizations have little reason to innovate because they do not have competitors generating novel ideas and concepts. They do not engage in innovative thinking because no other companies are doing so.

Additionally, the value of innovation is limited because it will do little to improve customer satisfaction. Customers have nothing to compare the product or service they are purchasing to, so they are rarely dissatisfied. For example, assume a pharmaceutical company comes out with a drug that partially heals spinal cord injuries. It is not 100 percent effective, but customers are happy with the results it produces because they do not have another pill that can be used for comparison. The pharmaceutical company has a patent on the pill formulation that will last for 14 years, so they decide not to put more time and money into research for a better drug. Again, customers do not complain because there is nothing better on the market.

Strategy

Most organizations have growth-oriented strategies. They try to gain market share through advertising, marketing, cost reduction, quality improvements, or product development. However, this is typically not the case for businesses that are monopolies. These organizations spend most of their time and money trying to maintain their monopoly. They fight legal battles to protect their patents, licenses, or positions in the market. This strategy is chosen because monopolies are extremely profitable. If monopolistic businesses are forced to face competition, then they stand to lose a lot of revenue.

Unfortunately, the maintenance strategy utilized by business monopolies has a major impact on consumers and other organizations...even if those organizations are not competitors. For example, the pharmaceutical company mentioned in the innovation section could formulate a better and more effective product to combat spinal cord injuries, but they choose not to do so to maintain their monopoly by fighting expensive legal battles. This means consumers with certain spinal cord issues have no chance of healing. Additionally, other companies that have the technology to expand on the drug patent are prevented from doing so due to patent infringement laws. This means these companies lose potential revenue and, once again, customers with spinal cord injuries continue to suffer.

Bankruptcy

This is one of the most brutal effects. As noted earlier, business monopolies control markets. When this happens, other companies cannot compete, and that lack of competition hurts them financially. Sometimes the impact is so great that those companies can no longer stay in business. When organizations go bankrupt, employees and their families are affected…and it can be difficult for them to recover. In short, bankruptcy closes businesses, but the biggest negative is the impact it has on people's lives.

As you can see, the impact of monopolies can be severe. Based on the potential downfalls, it is rather obvious that enterprises find a monopolistic position very advantageous. The next section takes a closer look at those advantages.

Advantages

In a perfect world, there would not be any business monopolies because those monopolies do not allow the competition necessary to continuously achieve higher customer satisfaction. However, a perfect world is difficult to achieve and, although rare, monopolies exist in various shapes and sizes. This is because, contrary to what they might say, leaders of organizations in competitive markets strive to make their businesses monopolies by preventing and eliminating competition. They do this because monopolies are advantageous due to the following:

Profit

Profit is one of the most important aspects of business. It motivates employees (especially those in higher positions) to work hard based on the potential for bonuses, makes stockholders happy due to return on investment, and allows for organizational growth and prosperity that stems from reinvesting. In terms of business, "profit makes the world go around."

Monopolies in business are typically very profitable. In fact, they make money at levels that other businesses can only dream about because they control their market. In short, profitability is very important to most organizations, and it dramatically increases when those organizations are monopolies.

Name brand recognition

When a company monopolizes a market, its products have the potential to become "household names." This makes its brand a permanent part of the culture, and it does an excellent job of advertising and marketing its products. For example, there are allegations that Coca-Cola is a monopoly because it controls some markets to the extent that people who want a carbonated cola beverage ask for a "Coke." While the monopoly allegation might or might not be true, Coca-Cola gains a higher level of name-brand recognition every time a "Coke" is ordered.

Technology

Technology is a double-edged sword for monopolistic companies. As noted in the effects section, some organizations become complacent when they control a market, choosing not to invest in innovation and product development. However, progressive companies think otherwise and invest heavily in technology because they have the financial ability to do so...even to the point where they are the originators of new products or services.

What does this mean? It means monopolies that choose to invest money in technology have a huge advantage in terms of organizational growth and development. Astute leaders realize the potential for this opportunity and capitalize on it for the future of their organizations.

Honesty

At first glance, this might seem rather strange. After all, how can honesty be an advantage for monopolies? The answer is, once again, because monopolies control the market. They have no competition, so there is no reason to be dishonest. They do not have to make questionable claims or promises that might be difficult to deliver on. They can tell the absolute truth about their product or service because customers do not have other choices. When organizations are monopolies, honesty truly is the best policy.

Pricing

It was duly noted in the effects section that price control has an impact on people and organizations. Monopolistic businesses have the freedom to change prices without worrying about competition because they control the market. They can charge more money for their products or services as long as there is demand, and this puts consumers at their mercy.

The above paragraph is completely true, and this makes pricing a major advantage for monopolies. However, these controlling organizations have the power to make customers feel good about their purchases rather than feeling like they were powerless due to the fact that they did not have any options. This is done by charging a reasonable price in order to make people think that they are not being taken advantage of when they buy the product or service. Again, this is advantageous to the business monopoly because a little bit of goodwill tends to go a long way in terms of customer loyalty...even after the monopoly ceases to exist.

As you can see, there are some advantages to monopolies. However, as might be expected, there are also disadvantages to this type of economic arrangement. These drawbacks are the focus of the next section.

Disadvantages

Business monopolies are advantageous in some respects, but they also create problems. This is rather obvious based on the fact that governments get involved to break them up to create a more uniform playing field. Without some type of intervention, it would be difficult to stop monopolies from growing into huge organizations that expand and take over other markets with their products or services.

The following are specific disadvantages that result from monopolies:

Exploitation

This disadvantage refers to the unfair treatment of consumers and potential competitors. Consumers do not have choices and are forced to buy from the monopoly, and companies that want to compete are unable to do so because the monopoly prevents them from entering the market. This mistreatment goes against the values that the United States has strived to uphold since the country was established...and it results in exploitation.

Wealth distribution

Contrary to what some people believe, business monopolies create an unjust distribution of wealth. The money consumers pay for products or services goes into the pockets of executives and shareholders...and this is not fair. Instead of having buying power, consumers have no choice other than to make purchases that make up the enormous corporate profits that benefit a select few. Wealth distribution is unfair in many economic situations...and monopolies intensify that unfairness.

Quality

Smart leaders of business monopolies understand that they have a great opportunity to improve the perception of their organizations in terms of quality because the products or services they are selling become very well known. If this opportunity is capitalized upon, then the products or services doing the monopolizing can transform the public perception of entire organizations to that of high quality. Unfortunately, this does not usually happen. Monopolistic enterprises take advantage of the fact that consumers have no other options...and the quality of their products or services deteriorates. These organizations have no reason to invest time and money into getting better because they already control the market. Complacency becomes the norm, and consumers suffer the consequences.

Bullying

Businesses that monopolize markets get used to having things their way. They like the fact that they have control, and the power they yield is sometimes displayed in a bullying manner. For example, a growing manufacturing plant that monopolizes a market by selling its product threatens to move its production facility to a different location if the current city where it is located does not change applicable zoning laws. This situation needs to be taken seriously because the city stands to lose a lot of tax revenue if the company relocates, but the threat is a form of bullying that likely would not be taken seriously if it was made by a less controlling business in the same community.

Worker wages

This disadvantage applies mainly to monopolistic businesses that manufacture products. These organizations control virtually every aspect of the manufacturing process, including the wages they pay their employees. Since many manufacturers utilize unskilled labor to make their products, they can keep wages relatively low. Unfortunately, this type of behavior does not have to change...regardless of the profits made by the company or the bonuses paid to executives. Union efforts help increase employee wages, but the fact that the workers are unskilled gives them limited chances for advancement or employment with other companies. In short, they must remain in low-level positions with limited chances for promotions or pay increases.

Now you understand some of the major disadvantages of business monopolies. The negatives involved with these disadvantages show why there is a need to prevent companies from monopolizing markets. High prices, reduced quality, lack of promotion, excessive power, and control of employee wages are all reasons the government uses its legal power to stop one organization from becoming too powerful. This leads us to the next section, which discusses the ways that monopolies are regulated.

Methods of regulation

How does the government stop monopolies once they are active? Essentially, they do this in three different ways:

- *Mandate price controls*

    Price controls set maximum and minimum selling prices for organizations viewed as monopolies. Maximum pricing prevents companies from unfairly gouging the consumer simply because those consumers have no other choices, and minimum pricing allows other companies to enter the market without the fear of being undercut to the point where they can no longer compete.

- *Transform private assets into public assets*

    This process is known as "nationalization." It occurs when ownership of a monopolistic company is transferred from private individuals to the public...better known as the government. Unfortunately, this type of takeover is not required to compensate the former owners, and it raises many different legal, ethical, and moral questions. However, the argument for this action is that the government will run the organization in the best interests of the people rather than the executives and stockholders.

- *Break up organizations*

    This action takes place to create competition in specific markets. Two or more companies are created from the same parent company to compete against each other and give consumers more choices. This also allows other organizations to enter the market because the parent company is no longer operational, and the newly created companies are not powerful enough to implement prevention strategies.

The above actions work well for putting an end to monopolistic activities once they have occurred, but they do nothing for the prevention of this unhealthy economic standing. That being said, there is also an effort put forth by the government to inhibit organizations from becoming monopolies. This strategy focuses on prevention rather than stoppage, using the following:

- *Merger and acquisition policies*

Antitrust laws are in effect for organizations that want to merge or acquire one another. In short, a merger or acquisition is only approved by the government after the potential for unfair competition is investigated. If it is determined that the merger or acquisition has the potential to result in any type of monopoly, then it is not allowed to occur.

- *Price monitoring*

    Government officials watch for pricing strategies that could lead to monopolies, and they intervene when necessary. These strategies include:

    Predatory pricing

    This occurs when one company attempts to control the market by setting prices so low that other organizations are not able to compete. Competitors cannot cut their costs enough to meet the predatory company's low prices, so they are ultimately forced out of the market. Large companies with vast resources are easily capable of doing this to smaller companies, so it is a big concern in terms of monopolistic activity.

    Collusion

    This occurs when two or more companies agree to fix prices using deception or fraud. By doing this, they are able to control the market and prevent other organizations from competing. The biggest problem with collusion is that it is sometimes difficult to prove or even detect. This means that it can occur right before people's eyes...and they do not realize what is happening.

    Retail restraints

    This occurs when one company wants exclusivity for its products, or it refuses to sell those products to the retailer. This is the most confusing price strategy because some instances of it are legal while others are not. This confusion requires knowledgeable government officials to sort out the facts and detect illegal activity.

- *Service monitoring*

    Officials watch for the quality of service being performed by organizations. For example, they look at safety records to make sure money is not saved by taking unsafe shortcuts. They also make sure people are treated with courtesy and respect. For example, gas companies are part of an "accepted" monopoly, but the government monitors them to make sure they do not shut off supply to older or disabled individuals who have difficulty paying their bills. The problem with service monitoring is that it is very subjective because data cannot always be used to determine right and wrong. In the gas company example, it is very hard to determine if monopolistic activity occurred based only on the fact that gas was shut off to 3000 customers. Some of those shut-offs might have been legitimate, while others were not...but it is hard to tell without further investigation.

Regardless of the effort made by the government to stop monopolies, they will always exist in small forms for certain amounts of time. Technology, copyrights, patents, licenses, brand loyalty, and location are all reasons for their existence, but it is virtually impossible for one company to have a monopoly...especially in the global marketplace that is present today.

Summary

Monopolies are defined as the "unrestricted control of the supply and sale of products and/or services." They are rare in the United States, but they do exist...and they prevent other companies from freely competing. Monopolistic organizations have a great deal of control over areas including price, supply, quality, and technology. For this reason, government agencies get involved to prevent and stop this type of economic condition.

This book focuses on monopolies in business. First, it examines the causes, next it explores the effects, then it analyzes advantages and disadvantages, and last it discusses methods of regulation. The text is informational and educational, and it is written for easy reader understanding at all levels.

Congratulations! You now understand more about monopolies in business...an important aspect of organizational competition and consumer satisfaction.

Accounting in Organizations
Basics for Beginners

Louis Bevoc

Published by
NutriNiche System LLC

Louis Bevoc books…simple explanations of complex subjects

Introduction ... 19
- Accounting information systems ... 19
- Cost accounting ... 19
- External auditing ... 19
- Managerial accounting ... 20
- Financial accounting ... 20

Functions ... 22

Methods ... 24
- Cash basis ... 25
- Accrual ... 25

Accountants and bookkeepers ... 25

Improving ... 26

Future ... 27

Summary ... 27

Introduction

The modern form of accounting that is known today is really not so modern because it dates back to before 1500. It was developed in Italy by experimental mathematicians, and that is why its roots are grounded in mathematics. It was designed to measure the monetary activities of organizations to see if they had more money at the end of the day than they started with in the beginning. This brief description is nowhere near an all-encompassing overview of the accounting field, but it gives a general idea of why it came into being.

In business, accounting can be broken down into several different fields, each representing an area of its own. These fields are accounting information systems, cost accounting, external auditing, financial accounting, and management accounting. Below is a brief examination of each field:

Accounting information systems

Accounting information systems (AIS) are used by managers who make decisions. They essentially gather financial data and process reports using computer programs. AIS are extremely useful because they are much faster and more accurate than people doing the work by hand. Add to this the fact that they have a virtual memory that greatly surpasses that of human beings, and it is rather easy to see why any organization that can afford AIS will never again make the same calculations manually.

Interestingly, early AIS were designed to process payroll. They were typically developed internally because software packages did not exist. Since these systems were difficult to use and maintain, many businesses chose to do accounting by hand. However, accounting changed after software packages were developed, and the manual way of doing things gradually disappeared. As businesses needed information from each other, AIS expanded into what is now known as enterprise resource planning (ERP). ERP is a favorite of financial managers because it manages all business transactions in real-time.

Cost accounting

Organizations need to measure cost efficiency, and cost accounting satisfies that need. Essentially, this field categorizes, analyzes, and summarizes costs so they can be controlled in the present and the future. Cost accounting is part of financial accounting, but it is mostly used by managers to make decisions about courses of action needed to monitor and reduce costs.

Modern cost accounting came into being in the United States during the Industrial Revolution. As businesses grew and became more complex, managers needed ways to control costs. This was especially true for manufacturing companies that had fluctuating variable costs such as labor and raw materials. Variable costs were dependent on the amount of product produced, and cost accounting could gather this data and help managers make decisions on a batch-by-batch basis.

External auditing

The concept of an audit is nothing new. In one form or another, organizations have been audited for a long time. These audits might not have been as formal as they are today, but they did occur in order to ensure everyone that the organization being audited was operating the way it claimed to be operating. In short, audits were used as a tool to evaluate and improve processes and procedures to reduce the risk of problems that could occur during business transactions.

Audits are an independent and external examination of financial transactions, non-financial disclosures, and any other aspects of the business that are pertinent to finances. They are quite detailed because their goal is to make sure all records, accounts, and statements are lawfully documented and maintained. Based on this, it is understandable that people who have undergone financial audits complain that they are long, boring, and stressful...all at the same time.

Managerial accounting

Managerial accounting provides financial and non-financial information that managers use to make decisions for cost-based and product-based planning. Specifically, this field analyzes costs in specific departments or areas to help managers plan internally by adjusting processes, making assumptions, and predicting what will happen in the future. Of all the accounting fields, managerial accounting is probably the most geared toward making predictions and estimates. This makes it useful for developing the strategies necessary to move organizations into better positions for growth and prosperity.

Managerial accounting does not need to be as accurate as other fields of accounting because it is only used for internal purposes. It is not required by law, so organizations can choose not to use it. In fact, many small companies do not use it because they prefer to plan daily. They are not looking at the future because their focus is on survival in the present.

Financial accounting

This field of accounting is probably the most familiar to people. It involves the analysis and generation of reports regarding financial transactions of organizations, with the most common of these being a company's financial statement (profit and loss). These reports are typically available for review by related parties, including stockholders, lenders, suppliers, and sometimes the general public. In short, the reports are available for people who have some type of investment in the company, and financial statements indicate its monetary position and value as a whole. For example, investors use financial statements to decide if they want to invest their money in companies, banks use them to determine the lending risks of companies, and the government uses them to tax companies. However, regardless of who needs financial information, it must be accurate to avoid serious issues later on.

Generally Accepted Accounting Principles (GAAP) is the governing body for financial accounting. GAAP includes rules and standards that accountants must follow when analyzing and preparing financial statements, and it allows everyone to view profits and losses from a common perspective.

Below is a list and description of important terms of a financial statement. Please keep in mind that these descriptions are very basic, and actual financial statements go into much more detail.

- **Balance sheet** – This is often referred to as a statement of financial position that balances assets with liabilities and owner's equity (assets = liabilities + owner's equity). The main components are often referred to as accounts, and these accounts typically consist of capital stock, inventory, cash, and notes payable. Each account has a dollar amount, which is also known as its balance.

- **Credits and debits** – These are the increases and decreases in the accounts on the balance sheet. A decrease in an asset is a credit, while an increase in an asset is a debit. Additionally, an increase in owner's equity is a credit, while a decrease in owner's equity or liabilities is a debit. The equation in the balance sheet (assets = liabilities + owner's equity) needs to balance, so if an asset increases (debit), then (1) another asset must decrease (a credit) or (2) a liability or owner's equity account must increase (a credit). This might seem a little confusing, but it is the way credits and debits are recorded.

- **Cash flow** – This refers to multiple sources of cash, known as cash and cash equivalents, which move in and out of a business. Positive cash flow indicates a company can liquidate its assets to settle debts, reinvest in the company, or pay money to shareholders. Negative cash flow means the company is not able to settle debts, reinvest in the company, or pay money to shareholders.

    In short, cash flow is an indication of whether or not a company's liquid assets can meet its debts. It also indicates the ability of the company to remain solvent. However, it is important to keep in mind that a business can be profitable while experiencing cash flow issues simultaneously because profit and cash flow are not the same. Conversely, a company can have large stockpiles of cash without being profitable if it is selling off its assets.

- **Fixed assets** – Fixed assets are formally known as property, plant, and equipment (PP&E), and they are also referred to as capital assets. They are long-term assets that are not expected to be turned into cash within the accounting year. Long-term assets include buildings, plants, land, furniture, vehicles, and equipment. Typically, these assets are in physical form, and they are reported on the balance sheet as PP&E.

- **Income statement** - This provides a summary of sales, income, and expenses for a specific period of time. It reports the profit of the organization, and it is also known as a statement of earnings or profit and loss statement. In a nutshell, an income statement reports the financial performance of a company for a select time period.

- **Profit** – Profit is a somewhat generalized term because it has different meanings. Some people call it profit, others call it gain, and still others call it net income. Regardless of what it is called, it is derived by subtracting total costs from total revenue for a specific period of time. It can be positive or negative, and it is often used to determine the financial health of an organization, which is important to investors. However, investors are usually more interested in a company's return on investment (ROI) since this is a better indicator of what they will receive if they invest in that organization.

Now that you have a little understanding of the different fields of accounting, let's move on. The next section discusses accounting functions in organizations.

Functions

Before moving into specific functions of accounting departments, it is important to understand the work that an accountant does in a business. People often think of accounting professionals as tax agents, auditors, and government officials. Yes, accountants do occupy these roles, but they are also employed in other areas of the private and public sectors. They work for regulatory bodies, non-profits, academic institutions, sports teams, medical offices, law firms, and other accountants. They perform different job tasks in these organizations, but they typically use their accounting knowledge to ensure that financial reporting is accurate and law-abiding.

In business, accountants play critical roles because they are at the forefront of issuing financial information to those who need it while preventing it from getting into the hands of people who should not have it. In other words, they are the gatekeepers who make sure sensitive financial information is only released to the people who have legitimate reasons to view it.

The numbers and figures produced by accountants contribute heavily to the progress and stability of the organizations they represent. For this reason, they are often among the highest-paid employees in companies, and they have direct access to top executives. They assist with corporate strategies, dispense advice, and help companies move toward accomplishing goals and objectives. Similar to attorneys, they analyze the risks involved with financial transactions and recommend courses of action.

One aspect of accountants' jobs that many people are not aware of is the potential for conflict in their job responsibilities. Conflict arises when their ethical values meet head-on with demands from the organizations that employ them. They can manipulate numbers to make their employers look better on paper, but this is unethical and potentially illegal. They must always exercise professional behavior and, as such, must do their jobs with integrity and objectivity while attempting to portray their employers in a positive manner. Unfortunately, this can be difficult because their actions might be contrary to those hoped for or expected by the companies that employ them. However, anything other than law-abiding and truthful actions would result in misinformation that could cause stakeholders to be left out in the dark.

So, armed with the above information about the jobs of accountants, it is time to move into the function of accounting in organizations. First, it is important to understand that most business leaders are numbers-driven because no other type of information works as well to describe the success or failure of their companies. These numbers provide information on sales, overhead, utilities, wages, materials, and many other aspects of the business. That information can be used to (1) generate records that indicate the financial health of the organization and (2) pinpoint areas that need improvement. These records typically fall into the categories of managerial accounting and financial accounting, both of which are discussed in the introduction of this book.

Accurate accounting is so important that it can make or break a business, and this is why some companies choose to hire outside accounting firms rather than do the work internally. These outside firms have one or more Certified Public Accountants (CPA) on staff who are very qualified and can handle most financial issues. The following describes a CPA for a better understanding of how they achieve their status and why they are needed:

Similar to attorneys and doctors, CPAs are highly respected individuals because they have education and experience as part of their credentials. In this capacity, they are licensed to provide accounting services to businesses and the general public. These services include auditing and the preparation of financial statements and taxes. CPAs also act as consultants in some situations, but this is frowned upon by regulatory agencies because it is difficult for them to draw a line between consulting and auditing. In other words, they become too friendly with their clients and fail to enforce the financial laws put in place by regulatory authorities. This potential conflict has resulted in many CPAs refusing to work as consultants and auditors with the same organization.

The education and work experience required to become a CPA are quite extensive...much more than many people think. Laws differ from state to state, but generally, a four-year college degree (or the equivalent of 150 college credits) is required before a person is eligible to take the CPA exam. This exam, known as the Uniform Certified Public Accountant Examination (Uniform CPA Exam), was developed by the American Institute of Certified Public Accountants (AICPA), and it is administered by a body known as the National Association of State Boards of Accountancy (NASBA). This basic process has gone on for well over 100 years, and it is unlikely to change in the future because it has worked well in the past.

The Uniform CPA Exam is broken down into four different sections that are all based on professional accounting. Each section takes about four hours to complete, and students can only take a maximum of two sessions per day (eight hours of testing). A general summary of each section is listed below.

- ***Auditing and Attestation*** - This section focuses on obtaining, documenting, evaluating, and preparing financial information and documents. Students must understand internal controls and be able to communicate their findings.
- ***Business Environment and Concepts*** – To pass this section of the test, students must understand business structures. They need to grasp economic concepts, measure financial data, and provide strategic direction based on their findings.
- ***Financial Accounting and Reporting*** – The third section requires students to understand the concepts, terms, and standards of financial statements. They need to demonstrate their knowledge of accounting and reporting for business and the government.
- ***Regulation*** – The last section tests the students' knowledge of ethical issues and professional responsibility. It also requires students to demonstrate their understanding of business law and federal taxation.

College education and the Uniform CPA Exam indicate students have a solid understanding of general accounting principles, but they do not guarantee CPA status. The third and final hurdle of the CPA process is work experience.

Work experience is required in most states before the authorities issue a CPA license. Some states waive the work experience for those who have the necessary education, but that waiver is fast becoming a rarity...and it might not even exist in the near future. However, the states that do require work experience differ in terms of the type of experience needed. Some states require CPA candidates to work in a public accounting setting so they can get auditing and/or tax experience, while other states allow those candidates to work in a corporate environment under the supervision of a CPA.

In today's world of accounting, it needs to be noted that most states require an additional exam that focuses on ethics before issuing CPA certificates. The AICPA offers courses to complete this requirement, but some states also require an understanding of their specific rules of practice.

Once the CPA license is awarded, accountants are free to work as professionals in their field. However, similar to teachers and medical professionals, CPAs are required to enroll in continuing education courses to renew their licenses. Traditional classroom teaching, self-study, and online learning can be used to fulfill the continuing education requirement, as long as they meet the minimum number of hours (usually 40 hours per year).

CPAs can lose their licenses if they do not abide by certain rules. This loss can occur from failure to pay the required fees or failure to enroll in continuing education, but those issues are often resolved with time and money. Much more serious reasons for loss of license involve unethical or illegal behavior. Examples of this type of behavior include failing to adhere to established standards, taking bribes, failing to act professionally, engaging in criminal acts, committing violent acts, stealing, coercing others, and making unwanted sexual advances. A board needs to decide if the accountants' behavior warrants the loss of their license, but the point is that it can and does happen.

Now you understand some of the job functions of accounting departments and the education, experience, and capabilities of CPAs. Let's take that information and move to the next section, which discusses important methods used by accounting professionals to establish financial records and develop reports.

Methods

Organizations need to keep track of monetary transactions to understand how they are performing financially. Without financial records, they do not know if they are making or losing money, nor do they understand which areas in the business require improvement. Add to this the fact that they cannot compare themselves financially to their competition, and it is relatively easy to see why accounting is essential for organizations. In short, information from accounting people helps managers make decisions that lead to the financial stability of their organizations.

Two major types of accounting methods that exist in organizations are the cash basis method and the accrual method. These are best summarized by stating that the cash basis method logs financial transactions when cash moves from one party to another, while the accrual method logs financial transactions at the time of occurrence...regardless of when the cash changes hands. Obviously, this is a brief and simplified explanation of both methods, so they are explained in more detail below.

Cash basis

When this method is used, revenue is reported when cash is received, and expenses are reported when cash is paid out. An advantage of this method is that it works well for keeping track of an organization's cash flow. Cash flow is important because it indicates a company's ability to operate and pay off debt. However, on the other side of the coin, a disadvantage of the cash basis method is that it does not accurately record financial performance information. This information is important because it provides a snapshot of an organization's financial health, thereby helping managers pinpoint problems and make decisions to resolve those problems.

Accrual

When this method is used, revenue is reported when it is earned, and expenses are reported when they occur. An advantage of the accrual method is that it accurately records financial performance information that can be used for decision-making. However, a disadvantage is the fact that it does not accurately track cash flow, so organizations are not aware of their ability to operate and pay off debt.

So, based on the above information, which method is better for organizations? This question is best answered by the financial people in those organizations, but the accrual method is sometimes required by outsiders because it provides a better snapshot of a company's financial position.

Now you understand two important methods of accounting used by organizations. These methods are discussed above, but this discussion is simple and does little to justify their complexity. Accounting professionals are needed because they understand the specifics of each method, and this understanding helps organizations see where help is needed. This raises another question. Do companies need to hire accountants, or can bookkeepers do the same work for less money? This question is answered in the next section.

Accountants and bookkeepers

This section explores the differences between accounts and bookkeepers. A discussion of this nature is important because some people question why an accountant is needed when a bookkeeper can essentially do the same job. In some situations, this might be true, but bookkeepers have limitations in terms of ability…and those same limitations do not apply to professional accountants.

Bookkeepers and accountants both need basic accounting knowledge because they work with financial information. Both of these professionals classify that information and generate reports using specifically designed accounting software. However, accountants take this process to the next level by interpreting and analyzing the financial information that has been classified and the reports that have been generated. Bookkeepers typically do not interpret and analyze any financial information because they do not have the education and training to do so.

Additionally, bookkeepers are usually not qualified to perform audits. They do not have the education and training necessary to audit finances properly. Accountants, especially CPAs, spend thousands of hours in the classroom and under watchful eyes to make sure they have the understanding necessary to properly perform audits.

So the major difference between accountants and bookkeepers is that accountants are more qualified to handle all accounting tasks and make recommendations that minimize risks and improve processes. In this capacity, they act as advisers for the bookkeepers who provide the necessary groundwork.

Leaders are always trying to make their organizations better, and that is why the next section suggests methods for improving accounting in organizations.

Improving

Accounting procedures add strength and structure to an organization if those procedures are used consistently by all employees. Some organizations, especially those that are big with multiple divisions, use different accounting procedures at different locations. This creates a headache for the corporate accounting team, and it needs to change for the overall accounting practices to improve. However, businesses that use the same accounting procedures throughout their reorganizations still need to get better. For example, some companies do not identify their financial risks. Their accounting people do their jobs in terms of tracking data and producing the necessary reports, but they do not look for problems…so they do not find them. This issue can be resolved by hiring CPAs because they function similarly to attorneys when it comes to risk management. They are trained to look for things that expose their organizations to financial risk. They recognize weaknesses and take action to prevent those weaknesses from becoming major problems. An example involves inventory. Regardless of the amount of inventory on hand, the cost is high if that inventory is not immediately needed. CPAs realize that this tied-up money puts their organization at risk for limited cash flow, so they take action to reduce inventory levels.

Another area where accounting needs to improve is the placement of personnel within the department. Checks and balances must be in place, or the organization is at risk for theft, manipulation of numbers, and other illegal or unethical behavior. The potential for this wrongdoing is greatly minimized when employees check each other's work. For example, at least two people should verify receivables to ensure they are correct and nothing is missing. The same goes for payables to make sure money is not being spent inappropriately. Another example involves the extension of credit. Someone needs to verify that credit is only given to customers who have earned the right to it. Something this important should never be based on personal "likes and dislikes" because a lot of money can be lost in a relatively short period of time.

Accounting can also be improved with speed and attentiveness. Receivables should be collected as quickly as possible to maximize cash flow, and payables should take advantage of the deductions available (such as two percent off if paid within ten days) to save money. To some people, speed and attentiveness suggestions might seem cliché and elementary, but many accounting professionals choose to ignore them because doing things a different way is more convenient and easier.

The last way that accounting in organizations can be improved is by using technology. This might seem like a no-brainer because, as most people in business understand, technology is critical for companies to remain competitive. It increases speed, simplifies tasks, and eliminates the need for people in many instances. These benefits are important for accounting departments, but they are not the main reason why technology needs to be utilized. A more important reason for the use of accounting technology is that it reduces the risk of financial information ending up in the wrong hands. Accountants can restrict access to that information and receive notification when someone views it. This type of technology greatly reduces the risk of financial information being leaked...which is very important in today's social media-oriented world.

The vast majority of accounting improvements require change, and change is not easy for every employee. In fact, the only change some workers can handle is an increase in their paycheck! Change needs to be accepted and embraced if it is to be successfully implemented, and this is best done using training and communication. Training helps employees understand what they need to do, and communication explains why they need to do it. Organization leaders must understand that the investment of time and effort will make their accounting departments better in the long run.

This section shows that accounting in organizations can be improved, and it suggests ways to do so. Next, let's peek into the future of this concept to see what we can expect down the road.

Future

Nobody has a crystal ball, so it is virtually impossible to accurately predict what will happen in the future. However, it can be said with confidence that accounting will experience steady growth for many years. In fact, accountants have a brighter future than most other jobs because their skills are in demand now, and that demand will increase as leaders become more and more reliant on the need for accurate financial information.

Additionally, social media today holds companies accountable for their financial wrongdoing. Companies cannot escape their bad behavior, and their actions can no longer be swept under the rug due to the transparency that social media provides. Organizations need to prevent negative exposure regarding financial problems, and this can be accomplished by hiring accounting professionals. So, in short, accountants will grow in numbers because accounting in organizations will become more important.

Summary

This book examines accounting in organizations by introducing the concept, describing its major fields, assessing the value of CPAs working within it, analyzing its job functions, defining its methods of application, suggesting ways it can be improved, and looking at its future. The text is informational and educational, and it is written for easy understanding at all reader levels.

Congratulations! You now know more about the importance of accounting in organizations...something every astute business leader fully understands.

Audits in Organizations
Explaining and Understanding

Louis Bevoc

Published by
NutriNiche System LLC

Louis Bevoc books...simple explanations of complex subjects

Introduction 30
Internal 30
External 30
Types 31
Operations 31
Quality 32
Financial 32
Safety 35
Ethics 35
Stages 36
Preparing 36
Gathering 37
Analyzing 37
Reporting 37
Checking 38
Challenges 38
Ethics 38
Workload 39
Technology 40
Cost 40
Summary 41

Introduction

Auditing is the process of reviewing records, documents, and processes of organizations to ensure that those organizations are doing what they are supposed to be doing and providing accurate information. In many ways, an audit is a risk analysis of an organization that holds management accountable for problems that have already occurred or could potentially occur.

Audits can be performed by internal personnel, but they are typically the most effective when they are conducted by external individuals (commonly known as a third party) who are unbiased and have some type of expertise in the subject matter. Internal and external audits are described below.

Internal

These audits are conducted by people who work for the companies that they are auditing. They might appear to be of little value due to the bias involved, but they are actually very beneficial when done correctly. Organizations change when processes are not working as designed, and this improves operations and helps managers accomplish goals and objectives.

Internal auditors look for record deviations and deficiencies using pre-determined qualitative analyses (such as interviews with employees) and quantitative analyses (such as a physical count of inventory). Performance scores are issued based on the expectations and priorities of upper management. These findings are often used to develop standards that are put in place to help organizations measure people and processes, and many important leadership decisions are made based on these measurements.

In short, internal audits identify fraudulent activities, unethical behavior, unnecessary risks, and ineffective management. When confronted with these problems, leaders of organizations must react, or their organizations could fail to compete in their respective markets. If audit findings are completely ignored, then organizations risk the possibility of ceasing to exist.

External

External auditors perform many of the same functions as internal auditors, and they are subject to the same code of ethics and conduct. However, unlike internal audits, external audits are conducted by independent third-party professionals to ensure the elimination of bias. External audits also extend beyond the scope of internal audits because they are more interested in the needs of customers and the rules put in place by regulatory agencies.

External auditors are usually highly qualified because they have gone through some type of training or certification process specific to the job, department, company, or industry that they are auditing. They provide a good snapshot of what is actually happening in the workplaces of their clients, and this provides generalizations that can be made about those workplaces and the people in them.

In short, external audits identify areas where organizations fall short of established requirements and standards. Auditors are independent of the organization being audited, and they are knowledgeable in the subject areas that they monitor; thereby adding a dimension to the auditing process that cannot be achieved by employees auditing their own organizations.

Like it or not, audits are now ordinary occurrences in organizations all over the world, and the demand for them is continuously growing. Many people associate audits with financial aspects of organizations. They are correct because finances are often involved, but just about any subject matter can be audited as long as standards or benchmarks are available for measurement. For example, ethical audits are becoming quite popular today. These audits focus on the treatment of employees working at organizations, but they also move down the supply chain and investigate the treatment of the employees who work for the suppliers of those organizations. They want to make sure factors such as forced labor are not involved at any level. However, regardless of the subject matter involved, auditors use systematic procedures to ensure organizations are meeting established protocols.

Now that you have a basic understanding of the concept of auditing, we can move into the next section, which discusses the various types of audits that exist today.

Types

As noted earlier in this book, just about any occurrence in an organization can be audited as long as there are standards for measurement. A comprehensive list of every type of audit is far too extensive for the scope of this book, but some of the most common types are listed below.

Operations

This type of audit examines an entire organization for efficiency and effectiveness. Essentially, it is a detailed and comprehensive audit with the goal of assuring that organizational objectives are being achieved. If those objectives are not being achieved, then changes must be implemented for compliance purposes.

Operational audits review organizational activities by focusing on efficiency, economy, and effectiveness. Auditors gather information on resources, time, and money so they can establish patterns, identify weak points, and point out areas that are in need of improvement. The data used to make decisions for improvement typically comes from operational policies and the success or failure of those policies.

This type of audit can be simple, such as analyzing one group, or complex, such as analyzing an entire global organization. However, regardless of the complexity, an operations audit offers new ideas and concepts for future risk management.

An example of a task performed by an auditor during an operations audit is to focus on one dimension of organizational performance. Performance dimensions include cost, quality, effectiveness, efficiency, work environment, and value, and the auditor chooses to look at the effectiveness of policy development. He asks questions regarding the process that management uses to change policies, including people involved, resources utilized, risks analyzed, documents generated, and time required. The goal is to find out if the policy development process truly is effective.

Quality

Quality audits have been popular since World War II, when military officers began to think about the importance of the quality of equipment in war zones. It was imperative for tanks, guns, aircraft, ships, etc., to operate properly when needed because human lives were at risk. A tank that did not fire was a sitting duck for attack by enemy forces, and quality checks beforehand could prevent this disaster from occurring…so quality audits were put in place for manufacturers of military equipment.

Today, quality audits can be administered in just about any area of business. They are essential for verifying whether or not organizations conform to established standards. They examine processes, products, and procedures and judge effectiveness and efficiency from a quality standpoint. They also indicate the ability of organizations to reduce problems and eliminate negative trends; thereby making them a great management tool for constructive criticism and self-improvement.

The global marketplace today is based on speed, quality, and convenience more now than it has ever been in the past. Customers demand quality and want to be sure the products and services they are purchasing meet the standards they are supposed to meet. The best way to gain that confidence is through a quality audit. Like other audits, the goal of quality audits is to point out non-conformances and push organizations toward continuous improvement. However, unlike some other audits, quality audits also point out areas where organizations are meeting or exceeding expectations. In short, these audits point out the good and bad aspects of quality in organizations…and some people find this very beneficial when always striving to improve.

An example of a task performed by an auditor during a quality audit of a job shop is making sure that preventative maintenance is in place to prevent production machinery from breaking. The auditor asks for written procedures and logs with signatures of the people who have completed the designated maintenance tasks. Lack of this documentation signifies a lapse in the process and requires the job shop to make improvements before it is allowed to pass the audit.

Financial

This is probably the most well-known type of audit simply because most people associate auditing with finances. There are many government rules regarding finance in organizations, and a major part of a financial audit is to decide if the standards for those rules are met or exceeded. Some organizations purposefully violate rules related to accounting to change their appearance on paper, while other organizations make honest mistakes that lead to incorrect documentation. However, regardless of the intent, financial audits are designed to expose monetary discrepancies so the reality of an organization's financial standing is accurately portrayed on paper.

Financial audits are important because false financial information deceives investors, lending institutions, government agencies, customers, suppliers, and employees. For example, an investment group might partner up with a company because that company is positioned in a market that appears to be ready to "explode" in terms of growth. This company is one of a select few that is profitable now, and the future looks much brighter than it does for those who are currently operating at a loss. However, if that company is falsifying documents to show a profit rather than a loss, then the investors are being deceived. Along the same lines, employees who work for the same company might look elsewhere for employment if they knew the reality of that company's finances.

A financial audit is best explained by listing the more common actions of auditors during the overall process. These actions include:

Confirmation

Numbers need to be verified, and that verification is only possible when auditors do the counting by themselves. Auditors cannot rely on counting by staff in the organization being audited because they need to ensure that the numbers match the numbers on paper. In other words, auditors need confirmation that the organization being audited is presenting accurate information.

An example of confirmation during a financial audit is an auditor who needs to verify the physical inventory of finished products. She goes into the finished product storage area and counts the number of products on hand, and then verifies the legitimacy of that number by matching it to the record given to her by the organization being audited. If the numbers do not match, then there is a problem in the inventory process.

Inquiry

Essentially, inquiry involves asking questions. Typical inquiry questions related to an examination of a monetary process during a financial audit include:

- Does this monetary process adhere to written procedures?
- How often does this monetary process take place?
- Where does this money from this monetary process end up?
- Who ensures the success or failure of this monetary process?
- What happens if this monetary process fails?

The number of questions asked varies based on the importance of the information, focus of the audit, and style of the auditor, but the point is that inquiry is a major action taken by auditors because, without inquiry, there is no audit.

An example of inquiry during a financial audit is an auditor who is reviewing the entire process of an organization's 401K retirement plan. He sees that pay is being deducted from employees' paychecks every week and transferred to individual employee accounts in an investment company that offers mutual funds, money markets, government securities, and bonds as investment options. However, he does not see who is responsible for these transactions and what happens if the process does not work as expected, so he asks for a written plan. The plan shows that the CFO holds fiduciary responsibility for the accuracy and legitimacy of the plan, and government checks are in place to monitor her actions. If the retirement process does not work as expected, then the CEO and CFO are held accountable.

Observation

A lot of information can be gathered by simply observing what is happening in an organization. The observation process does not involve asking questions, but it is designed to find answers.

Sometimes, silent observations make employees nervous, and they do things that they normally would not have done. However, after a little time, workers begin to forget about the auditor watching them and revert to their normal ways of performing job tasks.

The amount of time auditors spend observing financial operations is based on findings. If suspect practices are noticed, then more time is spent watching people do their jobs. Along the same lines, a workplace that appears to be doing things "by the book" will likely have less scrutiny.

An example of observation during a financial audit is an auditor who is watching retail cashiers take in money at their cash registers. The cashiers must follow established standards to ensure all money transactions, especially those involving cash, are accounted for so government taxes will be properly paid. If discrepancies are noticed, then they are documented, and corrective action by the retailer is required.

Inspection

Virtually every organization generates records. These records document internal and external business transactions, and they are useful when issues arise about something that happened in the past.

Unfortunately, the information on records is not always accurate, and inaccuracies are what auditors try to find. They inspect records to verify they are accurate, complete, and conform to established rules and regulations.

The number and/or severity of discrepancies dictate the amount of time auditors devote to the inspection of records. If records only have a few inaccuracies, then they might be overlooked to move on to more important matters. However, if there are multiple errors and/or evidence of falsification or fabrication, then auditors might choose to investigate further…and non-conformances will surely result.

An example of inspection during a financial audit is an auditor who peruses a financial statement to make sure generally accepted accounting principles (commonly referred to as GAAP) are being used and followed. These principles meet the requirements of the Securities and Exchange Commission, and deviation from them is a warning sign that mistakes are being made, information is being withheld, and/or documents are being falsified.

Tracing

Tracing is similar to tracking because both have the goal of finding something. However, tracing differs from tracking because it usually starts at the end of the process rather than at the beginning. It looks at the end result and tries to determine what it is made up of and how it got there.

Typically, tracing during an audit is limited to one or two processes due to time constraints. Auditors have a limited amount of time that they can spend on this activity because other important matters also need to be examined. One or two tracing exercises fall well short of a complete analysis, but the processes monitored provide a snapshot of what is happening in the organization.

An example of tracing during a financial audit is an auditor who starts with money in the bank account of an organization and works backward to find the original source of that money. She looks for a paper trail of transactions to verify that everything was done following government rules and regulations. If any step of the process cannot be uncovered, then discrepancies exist that could lead to non-compliances.

The above list is not all-inclusive, but it gives a general idea of what auditors are examining during a financial audit.

Safety

Safety audits are important because the risks they identify can save people's lives, while other audits are not capable of doing the same. The auditor often works with the Occupational Safety and Health Administration (commonly known as OSHA), a government agency that focuses on people's health and safety in workplaces. Machines, jobs, processes, and people are monitored by auditors, and non-conformances are issued for deviations from rules and regulations. In a nutshell, the goal of a safety audit is to pinpoint areas where safety risks can be minimized or eliminated; thereby protecting employees from physical injury and giving them the peace of mind that they can perform their jobs without the fear of getting hurt.

A typical safety auditor examines an organization's written health and safety program and decides if management is committed to that program. This commitment includes supplying the proper resources (usually time and money) for the program, assigning job responsibilities to those in charge of the program, determining the success or failure of the program, and making changes to improve the program.

An example of a task performed by an auditor during a safety audit is an interview with manufacturing employees to see if they are comfortable operating machinery and doing their jobs. These employees are asked questions related to their health, safety, and general well-being in the workplace. The auditor can then determine if workers feel that they can express safety concerns to management without the fear of retaliation. These interviews are also used to determine management commitment in terms of providing the proper resources (such as money for personal protective equipment, machine guards, safeties, etc.)

Ethics

This type of audit is saved for last because of its recent growth in popularity (as noted in the introduction of this book). More and more companies, especially those that are large, are requiring their suppliers to undergo ethics audits to ensure the employees of those suppliers are treated properly. These audits examine employees' pay, benefits, hours worked, and working conditions. If abuse is discovered, then the supplier must take corrective action or risk losing the business.

Interestingly, ethics audits also go further down the supply chain to examine the companies that sell goods and services to the suppliers being audited. If the goods or services come from companies that are known to violate human rights, then the suppliers will not be allowed to buy from them. Suppliers that refuse to abide by the ethics guidelines are removed as approved vendors.

In short, ethics audits are put in place to protect workers. This protection is important to companies that are known worldwide, such as Wal-Mart, because they have public images to protect. Leaders of these companies understand that poor images lead to damaged reputations and boycotts of products and services...which can be very financially damaging.

An example of a task performed by an auditor during an ethics audit is a check on the rate of pay for hourly employees who are working overtime, along with the number of overtime hours those employees are required to work. Overtime hourly pay must be at least 1.5 times the amount paid for regular hours worked, or regulations are violated. Additionally, some rules limit the number of hours worked in one day to twelve, so overtime can only be mandatory for four hours after the regular shift ends.

There are many other types of audits in addition to those listed above, but discussing every one of these is not possible in the scope of this book. However, the audits that are discussed help you understand some of the reasons for implementing them. Armed with this information, we can move forward into the next section explains the five major stages of auditing.

Stages

People dislike audits because they fear the non-conformances that might be found. The outcomes are never known in advance, but the process that takes place is usually routine and clear. In fact, the structure of auditing is sometimes referred to as "cookie-cutter" because it rarely changes from organization to organization. Every audit involves stages that, depending on the auditor, can be broken down into sub-categories. However, regardless of the sub-categories, the five major stages are described below.

Preparing

There is an old saying that goes, "Those who fail to prepare, prepare to fail." This can be said about many aspects of business, and auditing is one of those aspects because preparation is necessary to identify the non-conformances that are the major reasons for the audit.

Preparation begins before the actual audit is implemented. It involves the auditor and the organization being audited to define objectives and establish pathways to those objectives. This preparation is critical because it helps prevent the lack of understanding that often leads to disarray and confusion.

One important rule for the preparation stage is that it ends when the audit begins. People cannot prepare for something once they have started doing it...and this will never change. Good preparation is essential for moving into the next stage, known as gathering.

Gathering

Essentially, the gathering stage involves "fieldwork" because information is typically gathered in the facility. Sometimes this information is obtained during the fieldwork, such as observing employees' work, and other times it is gathered after the fact, such as perusing records and other relevant documents. Either way, information is gathered so decision-making can take place in the next stage, known as analyzing.

Communication is critical in the gathering stage. Without good communication, there will be a misunderstanding of what is happening in the organization and what records are needed for review. These types of mistakes can cause organizations to fail audits at later stages and, at the very least, add unnecessary time and expense to the overall process.

Analyzing

This is the stage where decisions are made. Auditors use the information that was gathered to decide if standards are being met. Standards that are met get checked off the list, but standards that are not met become non-conformances that require some type of corrective action.

This stage of the auditing process is often the most challenging because it can be difficult for an auditor to be completely objective when deciding whether a deviation from a standard is a non-conformance. Essentially, the auditor's decision-making is based on a risk assessment of the subject matter. Questions are asked that decide whether that risk is minor, substantial, or somewhere in between.

The following are questions that are asked during a safety audit of a facility where employees work with potentially dangerous machinery:

> What type of training do employees receive?
> Are the training instructors qualified?
> Are the training materials adequate?
> Are employees monitored or tested for retention of the training material?

If answers to the above questions show that there is a risk of employees getting injured, then a non-conformance will be issued, and corrective action on the part of the organization being audited will be required. Obviously, this is a simple example in a world that is much more complex, but it gives a broad idea of how the analyzing stage works and how decisions are made.

Reporting

The reporting phase is similar to the end of an election because results are given. Unfortunately, those results sometimes require corrective action...which is consequential to the organizations being audited because this corrective action requires money, time, and other resources.

Reporting is the stage where an organization is graded after the audit analysis. Typically, each section of the audit is given a score, and those scores are added together for a total score that indicates passing or failing. Passing an audit is good news for an organization, but the process is usually not over. All documented non-conformances must be corrected and prevented from recurring, which leads to the next stage, known as following up.

Checking

This is the stage where the auditor or auditing firm verifies that corrective actions and preventative measures have been put into place. Typically, some type of support is needed for verification. This support can be pictures, documents, records, or whatever else is needed to eliminate the non-conformance and prevent it from happening in the future.

Sometimes the corrective action and preventative measures require a series of steps. If this is the case, then documents showing what will transpire need to be submitted as evidence that the problem will be rectified. This action might seem like it is a way to get out of non-conformances without making the proper adjustments, but the next audit will ensure that the actions have taken place and the issue has been eliminated.

Based on the stages above, it might appear that auditing is a simple process that moves forward with relative ease. Unfortunately, very few audits go as planned with no roadblocks or barriers. This leads us to the next section, which discusses some of the major challenges of auditing.

Challenges

In general, people who have never conducted an audit give little thought to the challenges involved...especially if they are employees of the organizations being audited. They feel as if they are at the mercy of the auditor, with little say about what is considered a non-conformance. This might be true in many situations, but it does not mean that the people doing the auditing do not encounter their own set of problems.

Below are some of the major challenges faced by auditors.

Ethics

Gone are the days when leaders of organizations are not held accountable for their unethical actions. In fact, ethics violations are now at the top of the list of management problems that require immediate resolution. The public no longer tolerates these wrongful activities, and they will boycott products that do not meet their perceived ethical standards. As indicated earlier in this book, ethics are so important that ethical audits are now a type of audit that stands alone.

Ironically, ethical concerns are also a major challenge for auditors, and below are some of the reasons why.

Friendship

Auditors should be "friendly" with their clients, but they should avoid becoming "friends" with those clients. There is a difference here because friendly means polite and cordial, while friends refers to close relationships. As many people have experienced, close friendships create a bias that can interfere with objectivity. If friendship prevents auditors from being honest about their findings, then they are committing ethical violations. In short, a good rule of thumb for auditors is to never mix work with pleasure.

Bribes

Although much less common than it was in the past, bribery can still be a factor in audits if both parties are willing to partake. These bribes can be blatant, such as money handed over for services performed, or they can be much more subtle, such as supplying the auditor with dinner and tickets to a big football game. Regardless of the severity, bribes can distort objectivity…which makes them very unethical (and often illegal).

Confidentiality

Nothing is worse than auditors who cannot keep their findings to themselves. They are compelled to tell others about the problems they encounter during their audits because those problems are interesting and generate conversation. This disclosure of confidential information might be entertaining, but it is very unethical. What goes on during an audit is nobody's business other than the parties that are directly involved. Typically, this is the organization requesting the audit, the auditor, and the organization being audited.

Workload

As many people have personally experienced, workload can influence the quality of their jobs. Too much work means they have to put in less time and effort for certain parts of their job. If an auditor has too many clients, then one or a few of them will get less attention. Less attention to an audit means less attention to detail, and details are where non-conformances are often found.

Excessive workload for auditors is not always caused by having too many clients. Sometimes it results from having to grasp too much material or information. This inability to process everything is often referred to as information overload, and it can be very challenging…even to the point where auditors can no longer do their jobs.

In short, excessive workload takes away from the quality of an audit, and this is not fair to the organization requesting the audit or the organization being audited. Overlooking a non-conformance might seem like a good thing to the organization being audited, but that good thing is often short-lived. Problems begin to fester, and the next auditor writes harsher non-conformances that take a lot of time and effort to correct.

Technology

If auditors do not understand the work and/or processes of the organization they are auditing, then they will find it difficult to do a good job. They need to educate themselves or turn the audit over to someone who is more qualified. Unfortunately, changing auditors is often not an option because the more qualified auditors are working on their own assignments.

In today's global economy and ever-changing world, lack of understanding often stems from technology. Technology is constantly changing, thereby making it difficult for employees to keep up to date on what they need for their jobs. Auditors are in a category by themselves because they need to keep up with technology for several different jobs and industries to properly do their jobs. Obviously, this can be overwhelming, and that is why technology is a major challenge for auditors.

In short, some auditors simply do not grasp the technology being used by the organizations they audit, and this lack of understanding makes it difficult, if not impossible, to do what they were hired to do.

Cost

Like it or not, the almighty dollar factors into just about everything in business...including audits. Audits can be expensive because travel, lodging, food, and the cost of the audit itself all need to be paid for by the organizations being audited. Some organizations find that the costs of audits are not worth the return on investment, so they choose not to undergo them. When this happens, auditors are left without work, thereby making them uneasy about their personal financial well-being. When they are able to conduct an audit, they fear the organization being audited will refrain from future audits if non-conformances are too expensive to correct or do not make sense. This forces auditors to walk a business "tightrope" because they have to balance the needs of the company with the requirements of the audit. In some cases, they might not write up all of the non-conformances that they find, which takes value away from the audit; thereby creating challenges for auditors.

There are more challenges for auditors than those listed above, but they cannot all be listed in the scope of this book. For example, auditors' personal lives can affect their performance, as can their health, because, like it or not, it is difficult for them to leave their personal lives and health issues at home. Auditors might also have a bias against organizations because of who they are or what they believe. For example, vegetarian auditors might be harder on meat processing plants simply because they do not believe in killing animals for food. Along the same lines, religious auditors might give unwarranted breaks to religious organizations because of their personal beliefs.

Auditors can overcome challenges, regardless of the type or nature, if they try hard enough to do so. However, some are unable or unwilling to put in the effort, and that is one of the reasons why organizations being audited feel they were mistreated.

Summary

Auditing is a process that examines organizations to ensure they are adhering to rules and meeting standards. Audits took place in the past, are going on today, and will be present in the future. In fact, audits are increasing in popularity as organizations are forced to comply with more and more rules and regulations.

This book discusses how and why audits are conducted in organizations. It introduces auditing, explores the most common types of audits, examines the stages involved in audits, and discusses the challenges faced by those conducting audits. The text is informational and educational, and it is written for easy understanding at all reader levels.

Congratulations! You now understand more about audits in organizations…more popular now than they have ever been in the past.

Blockchain in Manufacturing
Explaining the Basics

Louis Bevoc and Allison Shearsett

Published by
NutriNiche System LLC

Louis Bevoc books...simple explanations of complex subjects

Introduction ... 44
What is blockchain? ... 44
Uses ... 45
- Data storage ... 45
- Regulations ... 46
- Data management ... 46
- Contracts ... 46
- Audits ... 46

Manufacturing ... 47
Food manufacturing ... 47
- Food safety ... 48
- Food fraud ... 49

Pros and cons ... 50
- Advantages ... 50
- Disadvantages ... 51

Future ... 51
- Cyber security ... 52
- Transportation ... 52
- Employee benefits ... 52
- Plant expansion ... 52

Summary ... 52

Introduction

Blockchain technology has grown to the point where it is now trendy to talk about it in manufacturing businesses around the world. This interest has transpired because blockchain provides complete traceability for products. Essentially, it puts a permanent time stamp on every stop (aka block) during the assembly of a product and then follows that product through to the retail shelf. In short, everything in the supply chain is documented, so if there is a problem, that problem can be traced to the source for resolution.

In a nutshell, blockchain is a record-keeping system where each record is referred to as a block. These blocks are linked using a secure system that stores information and makes it accessible at any time for anyone on the network. Each block has a permanent time stamp that cannot be changed. Notes can be added that refer back to something that changed, but the stamp can never be altered.

The concept of blockchain has been around for almost three decades. The thinking behind it back then revolved around the development of a chain of secure documents that could not be tampered with by anyone. Eventually, this early version incorporated "blocks" where data could be stored and transferred intact to other blocks. This incorporation allowed for the transfer of large secured blocks of information that prevented others from making up information that best suited their needs.

Blockchain continued to progress over time, but it had a limited following until the advent of Bitcoin. Bitcoin needed a way to log and total all of its economic transactions, and blockchain was chosen to get the job done. In this capacity, blockchain served as a public ledger for all dealings on the Bitcoin network. The subsequent explosion in the popularity of bitcoin thrust blockchain into the spotlight and led to it becoming the traceability choice for a variety of manufacturers around the globe.

After Bitcoin opened the door, other organizations started to look at blockchain as a security system. However, while this technology is a popular conversation piece among chief information officers in many corporations, it has yet to gain a strong foothold in terms of actual usage. In short, blockchain has generated a lot of interest, but most companies have not taken it past the discussion stage.

The above introduction falls well short of describing the complete history of blockchain because many people have spent countless hours working on and improving this technology. It has come a long way since its inception, and it will be adopted by more and more manufacturers...especially those that use multiple components in the assembly of their products. However, this introduction does provide a brief idea of the thinking behind blockchain, and it helps lead us into the next section that provides a more detailed analysis of this record-keeping system.

What is blockchain?

A full-blown discussion on blockchain requires much more detail than is found within the pages of this book, but the intent of this book is not to provide a detailed analysis. Instead, it is designed to explain the basic concept of this technology in terms of manufacturing so it can be easily understood by the average person.

Blockchain has been described by some people as a new type of internet. While this might or might not be true, it can be said with confidence that it has made changes to the internet because it allows the transfer of information that cannot be copied or changed; thereby making it valuable for business leaders who want factual traceability without the threat of it being stolen, altered, or misused.

The best way to visualize blockchain is to picture a spreadsheet that is shared with hundreds, thousands, or millions of people on a network. Every time a change is made to that spreadsheet, it is immediately viewed by everyone on the network, thereby allowing information to be shared instantaneously. Other networks allow the instantaneous sharing of information, but blockchain is unique because information is not stored in a centralized location.

Decentralization is the first important aspect that defines blockchain. Blockchain networks are decentralized rather than centralized, and this decentralization offers two distinct advantages. First, the information is available simultaneously to anyone on the network. It is not controlled by a single person or group of people who choose the information that is made available for viewing. Second, decentralized networks prevent hacking because the information is not stored in a single location. This adds great value because files cannot be hacked or corrupted.

The second important aspect that defines blockchain is its permanence. Once a block is created, it cannot be deleted or changed. This has great importance for fact-gathering when looking back on a process or procedure because there is no altering of what transpired. Unfortunately, it is not uncommon for people to change documentation so it is advantageous for their own purposes...but blockchain prevents this from occurring.

The third defining aspect of blockchain is the fact that it is digital. Information from the system is never printed on paper; thereby saving time, space, and resources. The digital format also makes sense because, as more and more people log information on the network, changes become continuous, and maintaining them in paper form would require an endless amount of time and money. Without a doubt, digital storage and sharing of information have big advantages over paper storage and sharing in terms of resource usage.

The fourth, and final, important defining aspect of blockchain is that it functions as a ledger that provides a simple way to verify transactions are real and accurate. It does this by recording the sequence of transactions in chronological order, thereby making all information transparent. In short, ledgers provide time-stamped documents that prevent fraudulent activity from all parties involved.

Uses

Now that you have a basic idea of the history and concept of blockchain, it is time to discuss some of its uses. Below are some areas where this technology is beneficial. Please keep in mind that these are just a few of the uses that currently exist, and readers who desire additional information should seek resources with more detailed explanations of the blockchain application.

Data storage

Many software systems store data, but blockchain stands out from the majority of them because it has a decentralized network. When data is stored, it remains stored and is never lost. Add this to the fact that the data cannot be changed or deleted, and it is easy to see why blockchain is a wise choice for many organizations.

Regulations

Many transactions, especially those that are legal or financial, are regulated by the government or other authorities. Blockchain provides transparency that is rivaled by few other systems, and, when combined with the truthfulness of information, it makes an excellent choice for managing transactions with regulatory or other external party requirements.

In terms of regulations, blockchain has an added dimension of usefulness because it can prevent people from being accused of or being found guilty of illegal activities. These illegal activities might have been conducted knowingly or unknowingly, but either way, the end result could be prison time for those who do not follow regulatory requirements.

Data management

Blockchain allows users to manage their data for several reasons, including (1) privacy of certain information and (2) selling information when it generates desired internet activity. This technology is so advanced that it can split data into fractional amounts for distribution to specified parties. Does this sound confusing to you? If so, then you are not alone because these types of activities are only fully understood by a select few people. However, the point is that blockchain is an excellent way to manage data by only exposing selected information and allowing users to benefit from that exposure.

Contracts

This refers to contracts that need to be "smart" to execute when conditions arrive or specifications are met. For example, a payout might need to be made when a company's stock reaches a certain value...and blockchain technology makes sure that payout is accurately made. This opens the door for direct interactions between specified parties without fear of mistakes or unscrupulous activity.

In a sense, blockchain acts as an overseer that might have required humans in the past. It can be programmed to factor many different variables into the equation, including legal ramifications, verification of identities, registration requirements, and protection of intellectual property. Contracts that are complex, detailed, binding, and irreversible need blockchain technology to ensure they are fulfilled as expected.

Audits

This refers to the auditing of people and processes in order to verify that the entered information is accurate and the results are meeting specified standards. Audits are typically conducted by third parties who might or might not be affiliated with the organizations being audited. However, regardless of the connection, audits are designed to ensure compliance with designated specifications, and accuracy and truthfulness are strong points of blockchain technology.

Blockchain has the ability to make everyone accountable for their actions. It can eliminate errors and stop the missed transactions that bog down many organizations. However, the goal of this book is to provide an understanding of blockchain in manufacturing, and that understanding starts with the next section.

Manufacturing

Blockchain is designed to follow a manufactured product from start to finish without missing any steps in between. For example, a company that manufactures tires starts documenting at the rubber trees and finishes at the time of purchase by the end user (customer). This is important because the stores that sell the tires usually do not have traceability at the time of sale. If customers complain about the tires, then a store only knows that they bought the tires from a distributor that dealt directly with the manufacturer. Therefore, the manufacturer needs to be able to trace their raw materials and know who purchased their finished products.

Traceability is especially important for safety concerns. Using the tire example above, a side blowout might require the manufacturer to know the source of the tire belts to fix the problem. There is not a lot of time because the tire store is under pressure for answers, and it might possibly be facing a lawsuit. An error might have been made when the manufacturer's supplier produced the belts, or the problem could have stemmed from the supplier's source of raw materials. Regardless of where the problem took place, accurate information is needed to trace the source, and that accuracy can be obtained using blockchain technology. With blockchain, the manufacturer is assured that nothing is made up or altered, so any information collected is real.

It can be argued that the supplier is responsible for all transactions that take place prior to them producing the belts and selling them to the manufacturer. However, there is no guarantee that they will have this information and, if they do have it, it might not be accurate or complete. Blockchain ensures truthfulness and increases the probability of finding the problem and correcting it so it does not happen again.

Blockchain is important for manufacturers because it excels at finding problems in the supply chain. These problems typically allow for the pinpointing of mistakes that other companies have made, thereby allowing corrective action and preventative measures to be taken. However, blockchain technology also supplies information for manufacturers to see how they are performing internally. This type of information is great if management is willing to take action based on it...but, unfortunately, that is not always the case. Some managers have "tunnel vision" or do not want to spend the time and resources necessary for resolving their internal issues. They know they might have to move backward before moving forward, and they are not willing to move in a negative direction.

Food manufacturing

Blockchain is beneficial for all manufacturers, but it is particularly useful for food manufacturers due to the wide variety of ingredients that they put in their products and the fact that people who consume those products can become ill or die from foodborne illness. The following are examples of blockchain being used for food safety and food fraud.

Food safety

Food safety involves making sure food is safe when it reaches consumers. Many checks are in place during food processing to ensure wholesome products, but sometimes those checks are not enough to prevent unsafe food from entering commerce. An example of a food safety issue that was resolved using blockchain involves a salad processor and foodborne illness.

Parnello Salad is a food processor that manufactures many different types of salads for food retail and food service operations. They purchase salad ingredients, including various types of fruits, vegetables, nuts, meat, and cheese. They use blockchain technology for traceability and can pinpoint virtually every transaction on the supply chain.

In the middle of the summer, which is their busiest season, Parnello received a phone call from the buyer at one of their distributors. The buyer indicated she received complaints from four different stores that had customers become ill after eating Parnello salads. She demanded answers from Parnello management so she could tell her customers what happened.

After using blockchain to examine shipping documentation, Parnello's food safety manager determined that three different salads were involved in this crisis. All three salads had two common ingredients….iceberg lettuce and Swiss cheese. However, other salads with the same lettuce were not making customers ill, so it was determined that the cause of the illness was the Swiss cheese. The cheese was tested for pathogens at Parnello's microbiology lab, and it was found to contain Listeria monocytogenes.

The CEO at Parnello immediately ordered a recall for all products containing the affected cheese. Blockchain provided the information based on ingredient logs kept for all products manufactured at the facility, and shipping logs showed who bought those products. In total, the recall affected over 100,000 pounds of salad.

Once the recall was in place, the root cause of the problem needed to be found. Blockchain was used to determine that the Swiss cheese was purchased from two different suppliers, known as Wingleman's Dairy and Jupiter Foods. However, based on the coding system on all products, blockchain showed that the contaminated salads only contained cheese from Jupiter Foods. This was good information, but Jupiter Foods buys cheese from two different manufacturers, Hartville Milk Products and Valerie's Cheese Processing. Blockchain was used to trace the cheese used in the contaminated salads back to Valerie's Cheese Processing.

Parnello was now certain that the problem occurred at Valerie's Cheese Processing, and blockchain showed that the lot number of the contaminated cheese used in the affected salads was 2121A. This information was given to food safety personnel at Valerie's Cheese Processing, and they began an internal investigation. After examining records, it was found that lot 2121A did not reach the proper cooking temperature due to a steam leak, but production personnel decided to use it anyway because they needed it to fill orders.

Blockchain showed that the steam leak had been repaired, but some type of measure had to be put in place to prevent a recurrence of the root problem (poor decision-making). This measure consisted of food safety training for all employees to prepare them for future food safety decisions.

In the above example, the food safety crisis experienced by Parnello Salads could have been avoided if decisions had been made with food safety in mind. However, this was not the case, and order filling was the overriding factor. The end result was foodborne illness and a costly recall, but the problem had little chance of being discovered without blockchain technology.

Food fraud

In food manufacturing, food fraud is the economically motivated adulteration of products or processes. It is similar to food defense, but it focuses on economic rather than chemical, microbiological, and physical adulteration. An example of a food fraud issue that was resolved using blockchain involves the United States Department of Natural Resources' investigation of a fish company.

An experienced Department of Natural Resources (DNR) officer noticed local fish markets selling a wealth of tuna to customers. Upon inquiry, the officer found that all of these markets bought their fish from Bluefin Foods, a large tuna processor with over 1500 employees. She went to Bluefin Foods and asked them for their production volume of tuna for the past three months. Bluefin has a blockchain system in place, which showed the officer that they produced 1,600,000 pounds. Blockchain also showed that the tuna was bought from two different commercial fishing companies, known as Beckman Fishing and Russell Harvest.

Blockchain exposed the fact that Bluefin Foods purchased 1,100,000 pounds of tuna from Beckman Fishing and 500,000 pounds of tuna from Russell Harvest. This immediately threw up a red flag for the DNR office because she knew that the catch limit for Tuna is 800,000 pounds, yet Beckman Fishing sold 300,000 pounds more than that limit. Blockchain showed that Russell Harvest reported only catching 800,000 pounds of tuna, and the DNR Officer realized that this reported number was fraudulent.

The DNR officer met with Russell Harvest's owner, Captain Squayles, and he stated that his people must have improperly weighed the product. The DNR officer wrote a report, and DNR officials ruled that fraudulent activity had taken place. The DNR fined Russell Harvest $25,000 and placed them on probationary status for the next two tuna seasons.

In the above example, food fraud took place, and disciplinary action needed to be taken by a regulatory agency. This issue was discovered because blockchain technology indicated there was a discrepancy with time-stamped information based on government rules that were in place to protect against overfishing.

Unfortunately, things do not always work out as well as in the tuna example because, many times, nothing is in place to prevent a company from making up information or documenting actions that did not transpire. If wrongful entry of data occurs, then "garbage in equals garbage out" results, and truthful information will not be yielded. For example, if a perfume manufacturer buys coloring ingredients from supplier A and lists supplier B as the source, then complete traceability means nothing...and it can lead to even more problems.

In manufacturing, "one up, one down" traceability refers to having documentation for first-tier suppliers of raw materials and first-tier customers purchasing finished products. However, a manufacturer's supply chain often involves many other parties that play an important role in the production process. The food safety and food fraud examples clearly indicate that blockchain is much more than a "one up, one down" traceability system because the problems were only identified after going further down the supply chain. For example, Parnello Salads would not have found the root cause of the foodborne illness if they had stopped their investigation at their two Swiss cheese suppliers (Wingleman's Dairy and Jupiter Foods). Similarly, the DNR would not have imposed the fine and probationary period on Beckman Fishing if they stopped its investigation at Bluefin Foods.

As might be expected, there is a lot of debate over the usefulness of blockchain. Some people argue that it is not worth the difficulty of entering data, managing information, and navigating the system. Others argue that, without it, there are no guaranteed facts because information can always be changed or deleted. This book takes the stance that each manufacturer needs to decide on the worth of blockchain based on the available information, and that is why the next section discusses specific pros and cons of this technology.

Pros and cons

As might be expected, blockchain is not "the land of milk and honey." In fact, there are negatives associated with it that keep some manufacturers from using it as their traceability system. Essentially, management of each company needs to decide if blockchain is worthwhile by factoring in the advantages and disadvantages listed below. Please note that some of the pros and cons have already been discussed in this book, while others were added for further clarity. However, the goal is to give readers a more concrete understanding of the blockchain system.

Advantages

- *External evaluation* – This is likely the biggest advantage for manufacturers using blockchain technology. They are able to evaluate every transaction within the supply chain from start to finish. When there is a problem, they are able to trace it to the original source, and that source is a starting point for implementing measures that prevent it from happening again. In food manufacturing, this traceability process is referred to as "farm to fork" because it starts at the inception of raw materials and ends with the finished product being eaten by consumers.

- *Internal evaluation* - Every organization can improve in some way if managers within those organizations take the time to examine their internal shortcomings. Blockchain brings internal problems to the forefront by exposing them to everyone on the network. This is good because it makes the need for change obvious and prevents the tunnel vision that many managers have when it comes to areas where they need to improve. In this sense, blockchain functions as a tool that removes people from their comfort zones and makes them think about growing their organizations rather than sitting on the sidelines as opportunities pass by.

- *Security* – In terms of security, blockchain is an excellent choice for manufacturers. It has a decentralized network that cannot be hijacked, dismantled, or destroyed. This anti-hacking capability ensures the continuous flow of accurate information that allows anyone on the network to get what they need when they need it. Security is essential for any type of traceability system, and blockchain technology is more secure than any of its competitors.

Disadvantages

- *Lack of understanding* - Blockchain is about managing data, and it needs the involvement of every department in a manufacturing company. Production, quality, sales, marketing, shipping, receiving, accounting, and other departments need to be part of the process for it to work as designed. If a piece of the puzzle is missing, then the input of data will not be accurate, and the end result will not reflect the truth of what transpired. Unfortunately, some managers falsely believe that blockchain is strictly a quality-driven function. They associate traceability problems with quality and throw it into the lap of the quality department, along with "get it done" instructions. Quite simply, this does not work because input is needed from every department. If the quality department is responsible for the entire blockchain system, then that system will fail...and management will believe that they spent money for nothing in return.

- *Data security* - One might question why data security is a disadvantage of blockchain technology. After all, a major advantage of this technology is the decentralized networks that prevent hacking. However, the problem with security is that data can be seen by anyone on the network. This is very concerning for public networks, and that is why many organizations choose to keep their networks private. So, in a nutshell, people with access to the network cannot alter or delete data, but they can use it for wrongful reasons, such as giving it to unauthorized individuals.

- *Resources* – As many people have experienced, it takes time and money to create work-related systems that contain valuable information and function properly. Blockchain can consume a wealth of resources, especially at start-up, and some managers believe that the time and money spent are not worth the return on investment. They choose to implement other traceability systems that get the job done with minimal resource consumption.

Based on the above advantages and disadvantages, leaders of manufacturing companies will need to fully understand the pros and cons of blockchain before making it a part of their supply chain monitoring process. This leads us to the next section, which discusses the future of this intriguing technology.

Future

Without a crystal ball, it is difficult to determine who will use blockchain in the future. However, it can be said with confidence that many business leaders will take a serious look at it because it has the potential to do things that competing forms of technology are not able to do. That being said, the following are areas of manufacturing where blockchain has the greatest potential:

Cyber security

This area of manufacturing where blockchain has potential should not come as a surprise to anyone, since security is a known advantage of the technology. However, blockchain will move well past traceability into financial areas such as accounts payable and accounts receivable. It will make financial transactions more accurate and transparent, and it will also speed up the process, thereby saving time and money.

Transportation

Transportation, which includes warehousing, distribution, and trucking, will be part of blockchain's future for manufacturers. While every aspect of the supply chain could potentially be affected by blockchain technology, transportation stands out on its own because it allows manufacturers to store and ship products without involving costly third parties. Time and money will be saved, and those savings will make manufacturing leaders happy.

Employee benefits

Major headaches for leaders of manufacturing companies include the benefit packages that they provide to their employees. Healthcare, in particular, continues to rise in cost, and it appears this trend will continue in the future. Blockchain can help stabilize healthcare costs by improving data security, speeding the sharing of information between medical institutions and patients, and verifying that information is accurate. In short, lower costs for medical care professionals will prevent the sharp price increases that manufacturers have been continuously experiencing.

Plant expansion

As noted earlier, blockchain ensures the accuracy of financial transactions while speeding up processes and procedures. This advantage will translate into savings in many other areas, including the acquisition of physical space for plant expansion. The transparency of real estate transactions will prevent errors and fraud while eliminating the need for paper records. Manufacturers need space to produce more products, and blockchain will expedite the purchasing of that space while assuring proper documentation is in order.

Summary

Blockchain technology is not new, but it has never been as popular as it is today due to the need for accurate, time-stamped, and irreversible data. Manufacturers are particularly interested in this technology due to the length and complexity of their supply chains and the fact that their customers are always demanding more in terms of information.

Blockchain technology is used by many different businesses, and this book explores its use in manufacturing. It introduces blockchain, describes its function, exemplifies its applications, identifies its strengths and weaknesses, and predicts its future. The text is informational and educational, and it is written for easy understanding at any reading level.

Congratulations! You now understand more about blockchain technology for manufacturers...a topic of interest that continues to grow in popularity.

www.ingramcontent.com/pod-product-compliance
Lightning Source LLC
Chambersburg PA
CBHW031500210526
45463CB00003B/1010